Making (

edited by

Ian Badcoe
Rosemary Badcoe
John C. Nash

Published by
Ravenshead Press

Introduction copyright © Cameron Self 2012
Cover image copyright © Sam Webster 2012
Design and layout copyright © Ben Johnson 2012

Copyright of poems resides with the individual authors and other copyright holders who are acknowledged in the credits on page 121 which constitute a continuation of this copyright page.

ISBN: 978 0 9571852 1 0
First published 2012 by
Ravenshead Press
The Lodge, Becton Lane
Barton On Sea, Hampshire
BH25 7AG

First Impression 2012

www.ravensheadpress.co.uk
For further information visit the above address.

LEGAL NOTICE

All rights reserved. No part of this book may be reproduced, stored in a retrieval system, or transmitted in any form, or by any means, electronic, mechanical, photocopying, recording or otherwise, without prior written permission from the copyright holders listed on pages 105-114. Ravenshead Press only controls publication rights from its own publications and does not control rights to most of the poems published in this anthology.

Printed in Great Britain, USA and Australia by
Lightning Source

*In memory of
Barrie Haughton*

ACKNOWLEDGEMENTS

Acknowledgements are due to the editors of the following publications in which some of these poems first appeared in print:

David Callin: *Piangere, Snettisham* (Envoi #16); *Mishearings, Morning over Chibbanagh* (Message in a Bottle); *Dead Pubs of Douglas* (Lucid Rhythms); **Jane Røken**: *Aubade for Edith Sitwell* (Snakeskin #174, March 2011); *Borderland, Shadowgate* (The Flea, February 2011); **Rosemary Badcoe**: *Elementary Catastrophe* (Matter #10 2010); *Drowning doesn't look like drowning, Boarding* (Orbis #157, Autumn 2011); *My Arguments* (Fourteen Magazine #13, Spring 2012); *Outlines* (Matter #11 2011); *The Concert* (Matter #12 2012); **Seth Crook**: *How Hebridean Sheep Walk in the Rain* (Message in a Bottle); *Angels Writing to the Hebrides* (Ink, Sweat and Tears); *Wet Morning at Mull Pier* (Snakeskin); *Crook the Gardener* (The Journal); **John C. Nash**: *Tales From the Bareknuckle Poet* (The Delinquent #18); *King Alfred's Cakes* (Antiphon #3); *White* (Antiphon #1); *Who Hangs the Rabbits* (Cake #5); **Brian Edwards**: *At the Kawamura Museum of Art, Haugh Lane* (Envoi #160); *A Secret Hobby* (The Journal #33); *Eating For Two* (Antiphon #1); **Lia Brooks**: *The Collar* (Loch Raven Review); **Lois P. Jones**: *Ouija* (Poem of the Year IBPC 2010, published in Raven Chronicles, 2012); *Picasso's Garden* (Cruzio Cafe); *Ways to Paint a Woman* (1st Place IBPC September 2010); **Ben Johnson**: *The Sloven's Assistant* (The Ghazal Page, Book Challenge Issue 2010); *Pantone 1660C* (2nd Place IBPC July 2010); *T.S.Eliot Takes the Turing Test* (Antiphon #3); **John Glennon:** *My Next Film...* (Aubin & Wills Spring 2010)

CONTENTS

Introduction - Cameron Self..9
Oblique Ascension - Jane Røken......................................11
Ouija - Lois P. Jones..12
Elementary Catastrophe Theory - Rosemary Badcoe........14
Feel Sorry for Mercury - John Glennon............................. 15
Crisis - Marc Woodward...16
Rather Cerebral Conceptual Graffiti Artists - John C. Nash.. 17
T.S. Eliot Takes the Turing Test - Ben Johnson................. 18
Outlines - Rosemary Badcoe..20
Making Contact - Suzanne Johanson............................... 21
By the Rising of the Moon - Jane Røken..........................22
A Secret Hobby - Brian Edwards...................................... 23
Who Hangs the Rabbits - John C. Nash........................... 24
My Arguments - Rosemary Badcoe..................................25
Mussels - Richard Moorhead.. 26
Gull - Kris Thain...27
Eating for Two - Brian Edwards..28
Feeding Time - Kris Thain..30
Mishearings - David Callin...31
Piangere - David Callin.. 33
Blanking - Ben Johnson... 34
White - John C. Nash... 36
The Year of Horses - Kieran Johnson................................37
Fugit - Ian Badcoe..39
Borderland, Shadowgate - Jane Røken...........................40
The Collar - Lia Brooks.. 41
Threshold Days - Jane Røken..43
Pomegrenades - Marc Woodward................................... 44
The Modified Behavior of Fruit - Jane Loechler................. 45
Pilgrim's Journal - Jane Røken...47
Baker - Lia Brooks..49
Slow Cooker - Lucy Iu.. 50

Table - David Kelly	51
The Dripping Tap - Cameron Self	52
The Sloven's Assistant - Ben Johnson	53
By the Book - Ian Badcoe	54
Tales from the Bareknuckle Poet - John C. Nash	56
Zen and the Art of Submitting Poetry - Cameron Self	57
The Concert - Rosemary Badcoe	58
My Next Film - John Glennon	59
Agua Potable - Jane Loechler	60
Angels Writing to the Hebrides - Seth Crook	61
Morning over Chibbanagh - David Callin	62
How Hebridean Sheep Walk in the Rain - Seth Crook	63
Dead Pubs of Douglas - David Callin	64
Corner Shop Cocktails - Kris Thain	66
The New Life - Kieran Johnson	67
Two Reservations - Suzanne Johanson	68
Egg and Soldier - Nicola Beaumont	69
Resolution - Kieran Johnson	70
Bed - Richard Moorhead	72
Wife - Phil Wood	73
Aubade for Edith Sitwell - Jane Røken	74
Picasso's Garden - Lois P. Jones	75
Pantone: 1665 C - Ben Johnson	76
Ways to Paint a Woman - Lois P. Jones	77
At the Kawamura Museum of Art - Brian Edwards	79
Necessity - Jane Loechler	82
Yin and Yang - Lucy Lu	83
Appletree - Barrie Haughton	84
Haugh Lane - Brian Edwards	85
Crook the Gardener - Seth Crook	88
The War of Attrition - Ray Miller	89
Boarding - Rosemary Badcoe	90
Taking Out Grandma - Ray Miller	91
Still Chartreuse - Suzanne Johanson	92
Split Second - Richard Moorhead	93

Bottom Dead Centre - Ian Badcoe.................................95
Snettisham - David Callin... 97
Omniscient - Geoff ?... 98
On the Down Line - Ian Badcoe....................................100
Drowning Doesn't Look Like Drowning - Rosemary Badcoe 102
King Alfred's Cakes - John C. Nash................................ 103
Just Make Sure - Barrie Haughton..................................104
Appendices..105
Index of First Lines..106
Biographies... 111
Credits... 121

INTRODUCTION

I launched the *Poets' Graves Forum* in 2004 with the aim of creating a serious place where practising poets could post their work and receive constructive criticism from other members. From the outset my approach was to honestly critique what was posted; some poets didn't like this approach and immediately left.

One of the first poets to stick around was Kris Thain (camus) and, in the early days, Kris and I used to work together to establish a critical culture and to encourage quality contributions. We were soon joined by a group of talented young poets from the US (Pseud, that girl and Absolon's Sword) and gradually things started to move forward. Periodically we'd get invaded by the 'love in' crowd or by raiding parties from other forums or by the terminally argumentative. Fortunately most of these people eventually moved on (or were banned) and, in time, the PG tone was established. In due course, more talented poets signed in and the rest, as they say, is history.

Eight years on - I'm delighted with this anthology which is published by the Ravenshead Press. All of the contributors have, at one time or another, been members of the forum and most of the poems have previously been 'workshopped' on the forum. The quality of these poems is extraordinarily high and I hope that they find a wider audience; they certainly deserve to.

Cameron Self
Norwich 2012

Oblique Ascension

This poem is not about you, in the same way
as it's not about the One-eyed Wanderer,
Finn MacCool, or Flash Gordon.
Faith is a fragile thing. We're obliged to believe
when we cannot see.

And it's not about bridges, causeways, ferries,
or ocean steamers. Stairways.
The old straight track, the winding country lane.
The world seems more than abundantly
connected as it is.

Nor is it about the exchange of messages,
by mail coach, courier, carrier pigeons,
or any other means. Especially not pigeons;
dove rhymes with *love*, but their nests
are carelessly constructed.

Instead, it could have been about travellers
who vanished around the first road bend,
or riverboats that left the surface and sailed off,
bands playing, into the night.
All their lights on.

Jane Røken

Ouija

"Green sunflowers trembled in the highlands of dusk and the whole cemetery began to complain with cardboard mouths and dry rags."
~ *Federico Garcia Lorca*

You asked for an R, for the ripening of olives
in your garden, the red-tailed hawk

angling over the road, the path
that took you down and away

from the empty room of the body.
The R of reasons, of the ringing that breaks

in a yellow bell tower – the only sound
after the round of shots that shattered

an afternoon. And the T can only be more time,
time to be the clock or the weather vane,

the twilight through your window
on the page. Your pen once again plow

and the places you took me
where I abandoned faith.

A is alone, how you never wanted it,
preferring the company of bishop's

weed and drowsy horses – the warm trace
of the lily and a flame,

for the night with its black mouth
that sings your *saeta*.

G is the ghost bird that hovered
at Fuente Grande that you did not wish

to come, for the grave some say you dug
with your own hands,

empty as a mouth full of snow,
as a sky that held no moon that night

only its pure shape to stow
all the names of the dead.

Lois P. Jones

Elementary Catastrophe Theory

Let us suppose a is alone, at equilibrium,
making coffee perhaps, or gazing idly at the garden,
considering the hydrangea. Tiny perturbations
can reset parameters. Imagine a scenario
where a picks up the letter, strikes a match,
drops the burning remnants in the fireplace.
Or envisage her reading, then regard the way
she hugs herself, unexpectedly cold.
Observe while a hits zero, the tipping point.

Let us have b enter the equation, walk down the path,
ring the bell. Our static outcome can leap
in an unexpected direction. a opens the door,
stares at b, but b is intractable, face shaded
by the trailing clematis. a does not know where
she stands; vary b, and the system oscillates,
attracting and repelling. She brings hand
to mouth, remembers now the lilies, soft
as fingertips, now the rough concrete
grazing her face.

The future is indeterminate where the exact state of a
is unknown. It may be that a will ponder past experience,
find it in herself to call the Alsatian to her side
possess the gumption to slam the door. Consider
if b holds constant and a vacillates; observe
the pitchfork bifurcation, a choice of solution,
neither of them good for a. b will rip out
the hydrangea, buy no herbal teabags. a will exist
merely as a derivative of b, a reflection,
scraping thick mud from her shoes, pockets full of seeds
she will never plant.

Rosemary Badcoe

Feel Sorry for Mercury

pock-marked
grey exposed

battered by solar geography

mathematically positioned
the wrong side of redemption

John Glennon

Crisis

Parked up by a wringing wood
on a crack-backed country road,
I shut down the lights and from the boot
took out a wrench: unflinching, cold.

I placed my mobile on the damp black tarmac,
glinting in the light from the open car,
and laid savage into the bastard thing.
I watched its shattered face fragment and fly,
numbers flicking out across the road.
I kicked the remnants to the side.

Lying down on the ground I saw moonlight
reflecting in the oily chippings;
felt gravel grit into my cheek.

If I could drive blindfold I could go,
avoiding all the places that I know.
Like driving in a foreign land
where all the signs are free of symbols;
faces are those of strangers, simples:
blandly unconcerned.

Instead I drove home, trousers wet from grass,
gravel on my cheek, to quietly explain
how I was mugged and someone
stole my phone again.

Marc Woodward

Rather Cerebral Conceptual Graffiti Artists
*a stolen poem**

I'm starting to wonder what is going on around here.
I just don't know. I just don't know.

Oh, god. You probably think I'm talking nonsense
                                         and perhaps I am
or is something else afoot?

I assure you I am real
                I'm somebody's cousin
                             oddly awkward, even ugly

I'd like to see a haze of
                random rhyme
You mean gutter as in sputter
                Catty rhymes with fatty, too.

My head is not quite making it to the page.
            is it actually injured?
It hurts and you get callouses.

Courage my boy
I've just remembered that
              water was synonymous with time
                         and "spadge" pulls them together.

Bentley, is that you?
I'm glad you liked the opening
It's quite Dada (if I understand what Dada is, which is unlikely).

John C. Nash

* All text shamelessly stolen from critiques on Poets' Graves

T.S. Eliot Takes the Turing Test

How close to sense his responses are,
almost lucid, almost clear,
almost what the judges want to hear.
How quick the switch from hanging men
to Shakespeare quotes and dogs again,
dogs that are the friends of men,
dogs that dig the corpses up, then on
to chess and games of cards.
We'll pin him down (*it could be hard*).

His mind moves to and fro,
through April, mountains, Marie and snow.

A babble bot is all he is,
a cocktail shaker filled with words,
a blend of English, German, French,
a mix of quotes and little sense.
He starts off well, begins to juggle
many thoughts until he struggles
and lets go his grip,
"*Twit twit twit
jug jug jug jug jug*"

His mind ranges left and right
through pubs and typists late at night.

A mountain stream that bubbles forth
with words from all the works of men
that gathered here from street and wharf,
from bars and books, from Lil and Ben.

A trick of language, sleight of tongue,
the flash that takes the eye away
and hides the swiftly passing bung.
A mind that simply cannot stay
upon the topic that we choose.

This is a bot,
            you lose,
                      you lose.

Ben Johnson

Outlines

Not everyone has words they need to say.
Some are content to let the boundaries of their world
explain: a hedge of bramble weaving tales
between the fence posts; hawthorn edging round
the lawn, white blossom concealing thorns. Here
a creeping buttercup whose runners planted tripwires
over rubble; a rumpled bed now filled
with bittercress. Some allow the past to speak.
Their feet sink through the soil into stone,
their song the rush of water washed through rock
where grit has whittled stories down to bone
removing all but ribs and spine. In time
the earth will slip away. By such means
the shapes of lives form contours in the landscape.

Rosemary Badcoe

Making contact

We craft stories to tell
like the radio signals astronomers send
into outer space,
not simply expressed sound
but words pronounced
in the hope of being heard
by someone, somewhere.

Monologue
after constructed monologue,
perfected and polished
in the same inner place
that propels us to move forward.
Motivation not from legs
or intellect's great schemes
but from that quiet place
beneath our breastbone –
buried behind the frailty that houses us.

Suzanne Johanson

By the Rising of the Moon

Write. Do it slowly, as if you're riding a secret language;
it's the only way to ply the code. The tower and the yew,
the cipher's nest in the willow. The lady of the fountain,
tiny gods that rest in the shade. Snake runes. A golden hand
with a blue eye in its palm: the sigil of forgotten causes.
New mythical creatures are being born all the time.
They are waiting behind the door; they are ready.
Follow their mirrormaze tales; they taste of iron.
Trace their longshore legends; they coil and jingle.
Their manifestations are clarion, cuneiform, casablanca,
cyrillic arrowhead, ogham, cordite, copperplate.
Listen to the lilt, the cantering unicorn, the inflexion
of the turquoise-golden forest as it paddles its roots
in the river. Rise the wind, singsong. Sing of the fighters
and the writers and the risks they ride: the very way
to name the game is parlous play.
But
for now
we should roam the fields in freedom.

Jane Røken

A Secret Hobby

We keep hinges in a jar shelved and sealed,
six degrees shy of sunlight. No-one bothers to look
or even ask about the doors, but sometimes

we lift them out and turn them over in our hands,
work the dust out of the mechanism, watch the plumes
in miniature caught in the slipstream of a second

thought. Holding them to our ears, we coerce
the holes to recollect the threads of screws,
to hunger for the door jamb's grain; with hushed

voices speak the long unspoken words –
Architrave. Mullion. Lintel. Stile.

Brian Edwards

who hangs the rabbits

who
    hangs the rabbits
        on the pine spikes and leaves
    their fur to felt
fluid to drain
    eyes hollow
        ears
            coil

impales the empty Tennent's cans
      fist high
          blue
              amid the brown

John C. Nash

My arguments

for consciousness in cephalopods
won't prevent you from slicing and frying.
I imagine three hearts (faintly greenish) slowing
and dying; watch as your fingers cram stuffing,
wonder how you're not seeing the resemblance
of you to that squid –

the variable skin that flickers and changes
to suit the surroundings; the boneless
writhing hastening escape. Its preoccupations
are yours; if you had those arms, it wouldn't
surprise me to find the subtle mutation of hands
to hectocotyli, honed only to harness
the female. I write you a note, and like squid
use the ink to depart.

Rosemary Badcoe

Mussels

The sea is hard on you – the way
it sighs at night. It swells
around your shoals of black shells,
drowns your choirs of silent owl hearts;
threads your towers of lupins, shapes
that have the geometry of fate.
Snatched in nets, you widen out
to drink the tightening, tightening wait
until I tap you and your twins.
My knife tip sees you are alive
in that impatient clamming shut,
just as old folk can't be made to like
a thing they have decided against.
I should ready you with bucket, water,
scrubbing brush and nothing else;
have cold insinuate itself into your beard
and my cracked skin with vinegar pain.
For that I'll make you gape with steam
and chives. You punish me with salt.
I love that, means I must add
more cream to smooth the broth.

Richard Moorhead

Gull

You, the lone fool
smoothed to an arrow,
tumultuously alone.
Wings taut, eyes
wind-burnt ablaze,
irresolutely afloat
in the sickening sky
awaiting the foulest of storms.
You, the lone fool
bobbing gently on the breeze.
Fat puppy gut – fish full
hauls you to rest
on the softened sands
eyeing lesser birds
harp-harking for tossed chips
like obstreperous clowns.

Kris Thain

Eating for Two

1.
When push and shove come, at last,
to stirrups and forceps,
protocol is waived and sans-mask
I take my place blindside of the mess.

First sight of his crown has them aflutter,
like pigeons round a bit of crust:
finally, right way-up, our little miner
tunneling his way into the hubbub.

If I remember right it was Trafalgar
Square, over a tuna-mayo sandwich
and a bag of salt and vinegar,
where you talked me into talking you into marriage,

a lunch-date neither of us would believe
would lead to me reminding you to breathe.

2.
Twenty-two laborious hours,
twice as long as her brother,
on an empty stomach too, unless
you count that brief encounter

with a tuna-mayo sandwich,
before the hollers wrenched me headlong
back to theatre, where my stand-in
was doing it all wrong.

At last, our little girl,
made of love, moulded by will –
I clean forgot
why my hands were cramped or what
it was they had been trying to shape
from your back, your shoulders, your nape.

Brian Edwards

Feeding Time

Leaning over the old bridge,
studying my silence, I watch.
Like breathing brocade
the carp – weave through mirrors,
fragment leaf-mottled waters
with measured gulps.
Summoned to the surface by
timing, by memory or perhaps

a distinct lack of both.

Kris Thain

Mishearings

A fawn, I thought at first: a sylvan scene,
of course, but Bambi-like, domestic bliss
embodied in those pretty creatures fresh
from drawing boards in heaven, full of grace,
unfallen, although that rutting flute,
sketching the diabolic interval,
seems to allude to something less pristine,

but not this shaggy fellow, sleepy-eyed,
awaking from his dreams of ribaldry
among the shrubbery. His jutting cock
is Adam walking in the garden, naming
the sullen nymphs and, knowing them by name,
sometimes pursuing them into the shade
to frolic for a while, and then subside.

Mallarmé is difficult. The grounds
include his *musicalité cryptique*,
syntactical inversions and the like,
but in his sonics, so they say, resides
a greater mystery, *ses purs ongles*
(her pure nails) becoming *ces purs sons*,
these (or those or his or her) pure sounds,

and in the realm of anecdotal myth
I've seen the same, as once in Orléans,
that hotel clerk and *Quel est votre nom*?
Yes, what was my no? Could Sartre say?
And later, when I asked *Où est le loo*?
Le loup? she gasped, and looked around to find
a chair to stand on or to hit me with.

Mishearing is creative. Ask the deaf.
(You may have to repeat yourself.) They work
with insufficient data, making up
their world as best they can from what they catch –
a state that may be general. Perhaps
the starry welkin rings with angels' singing
and we live too far down the treble clef.

David Callin

Piangere

Piange oggi? I'd reached
for the word I thought was right.
A heavy stillness in the air
and the questionable light
massing over Santo Stefano
prompted it. She did not stay
her clattering with breakfast things,
stacking them on a silver tray.

No, non piove oggi.
She was not forecasting rain,
an *acqua alta* in San Marco,
water in the aisles again.
Of likelihood of weeping, she
said nothing. Understandably.

David Callin

Notes

piangere - to weep, to cry
oggi - today
piovere - to rain

Blanking

"*There was no snow in Eden as I remember it*" Jen Hadfield

The roofs of cars
were whales humped
in the snow. Rarely higher
than minus 18;
gas pipes fractured, spouted
methane to the atmosphere.

                    Melville was the first to go,
                    Spine cracked back
                    dealing pages like playing cards.
                    The words burned on brain tissue
                    long after I called Ishmael
                    to keep us warm tonight.

It was Pompeii, but colder
we dug wounds to doorways
that scabbed in minutes,
scar free by morning.

                    Only Bradbury gave me guilt.
                    The image of the fireman
                    surrounded by flames
                    Itself devoured by flames.

The reticulated veins of power lines
contracted and snapped,
whipped fireworks
through the frozen air.

        The first failures,
        half devoured hunks of books,
        taught me how to part pages
        scrunching them into balls of fuel.

The carefully cultivated
layers of mankind peeled back
to this; roof, food, fire.

        We discovered the genius of Shakespeare
        could keep us warm for a week or more.
        The chapbook fellows only flared up
        full of heat, but no longevity.

What madness snaps the rigid bars
we crossed into adulthood?
Sent us capering in firelight
charcoaling moments of life
on the living room walls.

        I finally came to appreciate Selima Hill
        devoting whole pages
        to two line poems.

Men, unlike spiders, are unwilling
to curl up or curse God and die.

        The Bible shrank in my sacrilegious hands
        pared of obscure prophets and
        unrevealing revelations.
        Distilled down to the purity of ice:

    "So do not worry about tomorrow;
    for tomorrow will care for itself.
    Each day has enough trouble of its own."

Ben Johnson

White

I wake with the dawn and the fall
of frost-heavy beech leaves,
the secrecy of the night before
profaned by a pale sun.
The hawthorn wall, now gauze,
admits rime-hardened fields,
white and unwelcome.
Last night's embers lie
dead beside you,
the thieving air steals
your sleeping breath.

Soon the morning tourists will arrive
to cast their suspicious glances
and us as villains in their small worlds.
I know that I should wake you
but the town waits with stone hands.

John C. Nash

The Year of Horses

A thin sheen of frost glitters in the beam
of a streetlight. Nothing stirs in the murk
as I make my way to work in the early dark –
I'm the only one around; it's six a.m. –

flash of silver pastern and point of hock
vanishing into an alley like steam,
hoofbeats cloppering on macadam...
and it's over, quick

as the flick of a knife. This is in March,
then nothing until late summer:
I'm walking the towpath when I become aware,
across the canal, on a patch

of waste ground, of a foal and mare
incuriously cropping the vetch,
hemmed in by brick warehouses, each
quite calm about my presence there –

I watch them until dusk, when they drift
away. Now I begin to see horses more often:
on top of a multi-storey car park a stallion,
black with a white mane like spindrift;

on a Wednesday in November, a young roan
delicately picking its way through the weft
of traffic; and the cars are silent and the soft
champing breath of the horse the only sound.

That winter in every part of the city,
there are horses. A great herd
seems to be churning the charred
concrete into a rich fecundity,

but gradually they begin to fade;
for a while afterwards I see their sooty
shadows in my dreams, then pretty
soon the dreams, too, have abated.

I seek them in the throng, like Poe's
Man of the Crowd, and in the moments when
the city reforms itself: the time between
the opening of the subway and the close

of the all-night bars; on Sundays in the rain;
on the day the cherry trees
kindle in a Krakatoa of cerise;
and on my way to work in the early dawn,

but now I'm not sure what it is I seek,
or feel the absence of as I walk
the sterile streets and arid underpasses,
or what yawning lack
my ebbing memory of that year exposes...
what became of all my horses?

Kieran Johnson

Fugit

Above the beach are horses, or so we must believe,
having seen them lounge, tails swinging,
beneath the trees we strolled beneath
– the shade now only another belief –
when we kicked down through evaporating dew
in the imaginary morning.

There is of course no time remaining
the moment any moment's done.
Footprints on the sand lie,
another preceding one,
like a man saying "and before that I..."
all the way back to his birth
by the corner of the beach hut.

The sun westerns.
The tide erodes the beach.
We each stand at the end
of a line of our own feet,

pointing ahead to empty sand, a canvas,
page, or silence, lying pregnant;
the prints we are to make implied.
We know we will walk.
We even choose where the next few fall,
but beyond that know nothing at all
of what rock pools we'll peer into,
which breaking waves we'll salt-spray through;
except that the day in time will end
and we will wend back past the horses
– briefly real again –
with the seashore fading behind us.

Ian Badcoe

Borderland, Shadowgate

Unaware of the fact that they would never meet,
they kept inventing one another, in the dark;
each carving and assembling the other
from scraps of mythic skin, raw fragments
spiked with bitter tannin, mustard, blue ginger.

By daylight they built early-crumbling towers
offshore, and rows of lighthouses that were cracked,
flawed with songlines of the shifting shale –
but no bridges or causeways: too bold, too rash.

They exchanged fairylizard tales out of tabernacles
on coppery, hazy ground, smiling secretly
between themselves, by candlelight; each
the other's talisman, harpsichord against evil eyes
and cruel gods of uncertain denominations.

Far away, the rolling orange flicker of oil lamps.
The sudden night. The kettledrum. The edge.
The land lies sleeping now. Let it dream.

Jane Røken

The Collar

Bells send time onto the hillside after me.

It carries on the wind like a deep-throated crow,
presses silence away from the spire and cottages,
weaving between morning's hawthorn and trees
as I sit here on a fallen birch. Icicles sway

on the firs. A hundred colours of sky
spill through glassy prisms, decorate this eiderdown
of snow beneath my feet. As each light reflects
another bird searches the woods.
                                        He has sent them,
released their coiled wings from a cage
of fingers. Little black swells that grow
the closer they come. This man in his tower, pulling firm
on the ropes, is masterful – cracking sky like a pale
blue shell, pushing his shackle of beaks through.

Their caws will find me. Rough twines of string
under his hands are estuaries I reveal
as I brush the frosted bark. This tangle of rivers,
aged and earthy, leads back to him. I taste them
in the air like the bread he broke on my tongue –
dry and clean, as villagers lit a bonfire
in the Square. I heard them singing

as we spoke in the annexe. I told him the wax
on the candle was me – each time he burned
the wick, my blood coursed the sides, over his table.
He drew warmth into a hungry mouth, tried to catch

the perfumed curl of smoke leaving him
and pinched out the flame. I remember his body

moving across floorboards to find me, the same way
he searches now – desperate and wanting. He calls
through this stillness of winter, but I will not go.

Lia Brooks

Threshold Days

Mark well this moment
in the barrow and the hollow hill.

After harvest, before everything dies
for a while, the shadowskin that separates
your world from others, is stretched thin.

The reaper, the thatcher and the blacksmith
proceed to otherworks. Magic is strong
at this time. Spirits come close.

Links and burning rushes light up the alleys
between houses. The horn lamp helps you
find the path, it does not safeguide your step.

This is a friendsome neighbourhood, not like
other places, where your fellows may sell you
down the river. Who is your next of kin?

The country lets you dream, but wakefully,
of shrines and starsong. The birds of gods
take off from your roof, return to their own.

Wheels keep turning. Loosen everything
you once bolted down. You will be blessed
for seven harvests and seven winters.

Then you shall choose a road
you never thought you knew.

Jane Røken

Pomegrenades

The old woman picked "Pomegrenades"
carefully holding the handle, securing the pin,
she placed them in her basket.
Gingerly avoiding the land mines,
she moved down to the salad garden. The rocket
launchers were growing tall: higher than last year's bazookas.
She heard a blackbird sing from somewhere within
the camouflage netting cast over the fruit cage.
The vine was heavy with bullets: ("Grapes Of Rage");
she must return with her trug and a magazine.
The nail bombs like spikey artichokes – "Jerusalem"
it said on the tag: she placed one into a bag.
Looking at the sky she felt the dusk
cosseting in. She should pop to the shop
before it got dark. Light the fire, think about tea.
Leaving the garden locked up securely

Marc Woodward

The Modified Behavior of Fruit

The motherland can tell
the apples are insincere
which she takes personally

but the trees stand up,
urge her to deliver
a not-guilty verdict.

I climb to add my forensics
and objections, a well rehearsed
pretending not to know.

I've been cutting teeth
in chambers. Emptying trash.
Coordinating hand and eye.

There will be no hearing
to suppress her findings. I fall
on calloused knees

into the rotting brown
bruise pile amongst wasps
and codling moth larvae.

I'll have nothing to do
with temptation.
I'm not your ordinary folderol.

When I have no more need
for her mercy I'll be gone
for good, down a wonky path

of bottlenecks and hairpins
with a pocketful of beans
for a giant, a campfire

for a cowboy, worm bedding
for a farmer, and a password
for the Pauper King.

Jane Loechler

Pilgrim's Journal

On the forty-first day of the nineteenth month
I pack up my bags and tiptoe down
the long spiral ladder from the Baybell tower.

Up the ginnel I go, through the snicket,
past the stubborn skerry where ships come to grief.
The morning is cool and vague,
every bird's cry muted, weighty and symbolic:
weeka weeka weeka fen fen fen fenugreek.

I follow the directions I've been given,
confident of their importance, their cants divine;
they lead me down the cove to the boatshed,
its door sagging on old leather hinges.

There, in a metal chest lies a hidebound book, big,
black enough and heavy enough to sink a clipper.
I don't want to wake it up. I leave it alone.

Out of another chest comes the little skiff.
I take it to the water. Its banyan sail blows me
across Octopus Bay, towards Funnel Island.

Wavelets cluck me on. I rehearse passwords
and signs, and sayings that have power and effect:
weeka weeka weeka fen fen fenugreek.

When at last I tumble out of my leaky coracle, tired,
thirsty, more dead than alive, I have the good luck
to join a small band of Zogairy pilgrims.

We proceed to the Temple Pit. We strike camp
and worship. We burrow into the red sand, meditate,
sacrifice, count to ten, or fourteen, or a hundred,
and worship some more: *weeka weeka weeka fen.*

Soon the place is filling up with preachers,
griffers, and devouties. The slopes settle so smoothly
around them. Yet they're becoming restless,
crazed eyes swishing back and forth, excess arms
flailing like mobs of giant squid.

The bottom-feeders will want their sacraments.
As I leave, the sky begins to redden.

All the long way home I'm being stalked
by a travelling prophet known as The Unsleeping Eye.
Unredeemed, I stick to the towpath as far as I can.
Weeka weeka weeka fen fen fen fenugreek.

Jane Røken

Baker

From the larder, mother, behind the door
which you painted duck-egg,
I have taken the sour water
off the top of the goats' cheese, the yeast
from its twist of paper, and the leftovers
of the butter-flour worked
through your long fingers with a salt-
pinch, the rest over your shoulder.

And the bowl with the chip and crack,
its calligraphy line browning,
I've taken it down from the dresser,
used it like a witch
over her caldron, dropping in creatures
too small for the naked eye. And now I am waiting
for their drama. Casting spells over them,
having them rise up and be noticed. I'm afraid

of them, mother, of what I have done –
swelling them like the throats of toads, oversized
and all wrong, just so I can see them... just once
so I can look at them squarely and say,
I have turned you to food,
now I can swallow you down.

Lia Brooks

Slow Cooker

Today I want to say something wonderful
about my slow cooker –
a Rival, a crock nestled
in stainless steel shell,
when heated, it simmers like hot springs.

I want to tell you how mild tempered it is –
you throw in beef tendon, carrots,
kidney beans, shiitake and kelp...
add hot water and aniseeds,
turn the switch
and leave it to hatch.
Go read, relax, or run an errand.
When you return, you'll see how
soft fire makes tender meat.

I love the way steam whistles softly,
pushing the glass lid that gently pops
poof, poof, poof to the rhythm of bubbling
stews. No spills, but an escape of aroma;

inside, everything dissolves in a slow burn.

Lucy Lu

Table

The past's engrained
upon your face.
None can deny your age
or grace;
a lifestyle with a steady pace
left you standing tall.

But blind cupidity
breeds true; deep forest
couldn't shelter you.
They sought your heart
and ran it through;
brought you to your knees.

Now balanced on
another's feet
as ape-like mayflies
sit to eat,
the ignominy is complete,
but death still has its splinters.

David Kelly

The Dripping Tap

On the tap-end
A water droplet is forming
Imperceptibly –
Its tiny globe glistening
And its meniscus
Starting to stretch under the
Weight of its water –
But for this brief moment it
Hangs defiantly
Above the sink's hard steel –
Lit up like molten metal.

Cameron Self

The Sloven's Assistant

"I help the auctioneer, the sloven does not half know his business." - Walt Whitman

Long before they came to me they slipped off their jackets
comfortable in the colour of their skins.

Each had two tales to tell, the one written within
the other told in scars, stains, odours of former owners.

I touch them gently running fingers along spines
wrinkled like a bird's whose wings are bent back.

I used to line them up by name, they looked unruly
now I rank them by size and shape, pleasing on the eye.

Buyers come to seek only the perfect examples
ignoring the passions, desires or aspirations within.

Maybe I should liberate the wretches, drive them to the streets
to sleep in doorways, the rain pulping them into obscurity.

But without them what do I become?
A man hunched over staring at empty palms.

Ben Johnson

By the Book

She reads books,
this is where it all begins.
"Planning the crime of the century,"
was just a way to pass a rainy day
in the library
in Kidderminster

but here she is
leading *Crusher*, *Sparks* and *The Countess*
through the British Museum at three a.m.
with a silenced pallet truck.

>He reads books
this is how it all begins.
He read "Lives of The Real Detectives,"
which seemed harmless enough
waiting for the 7:15.

>The radio coughs nervously,
a glance at Constable Granger,
a nod to Dave from the Art Squad.
They've all seen the shadows moving
behind the glass.

She's read: "Alarm Systems Explained."

>He's studied:
"Weakness of the Criminal Mind"
at some length.

"Transport of Art Treasures."

                "Traps – their design and construction,"

"The Great Escapologists."

                "Anatomy of a Manhunt."

"Losing Yourself in London."

                "Forensics for Beginners."

        An abandoned factory in Croydon –
            armed police converge.

But she's memorised:
"Victorian Sewers Revealed."

                    And he's left
                flipping the pages
           of "Sealed Room Mysteries,
                      Volume 4."

She opens a small bookshop.

                    He's in there buying
              "Should you Trust Books?"

        They nod.

Ian Badcoe

Tales from the Bareknuckle Poet

...and then there was the time I was up against Armitage in the Featherweight poetry title fight.

It was in the underground car park of an abandoned inner-city library, round the back by the book bins. An audience half made up of bespectacled literary critics and half of the chucking out time hoi-polloi.

The ring was hastily made from early Penguin paperback discards. I eyed him in the blue corner (biographies), the Yorkshire Kid with his Hacienda haircut, bobbing and weaving as he warmed up with a few rhyming couplets, while I sat in the red corner (drama) reciting the likes of Betjeman under my breath, watching his form.

Seconds out, round one and he was there with an incessant jab, jab, jab of monotone quatrains. I countered them with a couple of carefully considered quatrains of my own, with full alliteration. That confused him for a minute, but then Bam! – a sonnet to the spleen and I was stunned. Then he floored me with his stories, they came thick and fast, thick and fast until I wound up down and out and seeing stars.

John C. Nash

Zen and the Art of Submitting Poetry

Rejection does not make you a bad poet.
Acceptance does not make you a good one.
Therefore, neither should trouble you.

Chase after fame, however, and you put your life
Into the hands of others:
They will tip you between hope and despair.

Aim, then, to be aimless.
Seek neither publication, nor acclaim:
Submit without submitting.

Cameron Self

The Concert

Hendrick ter Brugghen (1626)

Intense as a conspiracy, coiled
and drawn into the corner:
three musicians, a single candle.

The boy sings the beating of their blood,
hand focussed on the fall of notes,
eyes sightless past the taper's glow.

The flautist knows falling dark upon his neck;
swings with fingers raised to scrutinise the room
across the starry glint of grapes.

Hair bound in white, the third turns light
upon her cheek and twists, lips parted.
Air moves uneasily, dust motes

stirred at the rise of song, disturbed
by the crack of secret papers
bound into the softness of their sleeves,

the vial of poison slipped
beneath the cover of a lute,
dripped into red Venetian wine.

Rosemary Badcoe

My Next Film...

will have a bearded left wing protagonist
raging on behalf of the proletariat.

He'll share a flat with a metaphor for the 21st century malaise

and when they talk

they will talk in the forgotten syntax of washing powder ads
from the 50's and construct sentences from toilet graffiti
remembered from youth.

Their flat will be infested with insects and disgruntled
middle management,
grumbling about the lack of vertical opportunities
and the implementation of a new computer system.

Filing cabinets will contain stolen secrets of unknown cultures,
manilla folders will hold evidence of unsolved murder cases
stretching back a hundred years where the suspects all look
uncannily the same.

The theory of a time travelling murderer is considered
but never openly discussed.

The fridge contains nothing but under developed
ideas and stale rhetoric.

This is a flat with no doors.

John Glennon

Agua Potable

On a chair built for vaudeville
I drink water color.
You take your coffee,
by black you mean black.

We are a revue of sight gags,
spinning columns of newspaper
words. Ink and rollers
drum between us.

I sing like a chickadee
until your pistol says BANG
in finger quotes.

Everything is left.
Your wife, her money.
On the table, a few bristles sink
into an asterisk
at the bottom of the cup.

I keep my footnote
in my mouth. My brush
is loaded, ready to bloom.

Hellzapoppin' but the rain comes
in biblical proportion. I hold my mark
with one eye on the shepherd's crook
reaching from off stage
for your neck.

Jane Loechler

Angels Writing to the Hebrides

Madam,
there has been
a misunderstanding,
a misapprehension,
something of that sort.
Although we angels do drop daily
to the heather,
it is not a question of
bad oxygen supply.
No, we like it.
It is probably a sexual thing.
We like to bounce on
our bottoms.
Of course for you humans
heather is not the thing.
Your lot prefer pillows,
rubber, elephants and such.
But we're made of angel flesh
and it is not susceptible
to scratches, itches.
I hope that clears the matter up.
Although we should add
that we do not like lichen.
That is a bounce too far.
We leave you to that in
– Where?
– Isle of Snull, Gull, Drull, Mull?
Yours, Angels

Seth Crook

Morning Over Chibbanagh

Across a pale December sky,
as pretty as a fan,
whose colours seem to reify
a mythical Japan,

there pass two solitary birds:
a lost quotation mark
trying to find its flock of words
before the page grows dark.

David Callin

How Hebridean Sheep Walk in the Rain

Warmed only by the red dye on their backs,
they walk as fishermen
who've lost their creels; and so –

must waddle for a trade
and, wordless, in unsuited toes,
mourn in silences beyond all reels.

Seth Crook

Dead Pubs of Douglas

We will not start
with a couple in the Star
before moving on
to the Theatre Royal
with its peculiar booths
reminiscent of third class rail travel.

We will not mingle
with what passes for Bohemia
in the Dogs' Home, or tackle
the strenuous itinerary
of the Barbary Coast,
the gaudy quayside establishments.

We will not be barred
from the Grosvenor,
nor will we be called
a dickhead into the bargain;
even these old courtesies
are no longer extended.

The lost pubs of Douglas: let
me memorialise them here –
the Ridgeway, the Railway, the Wheatsheaf,
the Globe, the Raglan, the Shakespeare:
where are your smoke-stained ceilings?
Where are the snugs of yesteryear?

And if some phantom barman,
having taken our pence
and draped the towels over the pumps,
should ask, in a spirit of waggery,
if we have no homes to go to,
we'll start to say we do, then stop and wonder.

David Callin

Corner Shop Cocktails

Shall I mourn your decline with some ad-hoc wine?
Or perhaps sip from Black Tower in my darkest
of hours? Corner shop cocktails bind the poor drinker,

the lonesome celebrator; bind them to park bench parties,
and bandstand barnies – wild stuff amongst the pond lilies
and hyper-green duck shit. Charity coats from the dead

flap about, whilst drunks on missions, go pissing, on the
lawn green-green, of the lawn green bowls club. And
how I remember your magic woman hands casting

spells upon my thighs, as we shivered the ice off the special
brew surprise, in that bus station that charged for a hard floor
and a gin. You serviced me through four layers:

My special half hour I called it, *a luke-warm-wank*
you called it, and we laughed into unconsciousness.
Next day we meet for cocktails, same time, same place,
different people.

Kris Thain

The New Life

Easter Sunday is the day I associate with you,
because that day I shambled through Battersea,
a man trapped fast between a fast-moving new
love and an old, and few men have a gait flat as he:
and that was me (the Albert Bridge frostily twinkling)
entering Chelsea, the previous unprofitable year
manacling me by the ankles. But an inkling
of better luck. And in a shadow the shop of a chocolatier

ablaze with light and luscious caramel and rose-
coloured wrapping and ribbon, and I walked in:
alone, as though on a vast steppe (except I suppose
for the merchant himself). And then I balked: in
a splendid cabinet rested an array of eggs,
dense and dark and sparkling, and muraled round
with incantations long and lovely as your legs,
and more intricately patterned and profound

than the river I'd just traversed.
I spent about a hundred quid, I think (it felt
like more at the time). As I left the shop a burst
of cold wind hit me and sunlight fell full-pelt
and I knew I was right to give up my old existence.
I walked back to your flat on Cambridge Rd.,
it was two, ten, a hundred miles, it was any distance,
it was SW11, it was Narnia, it was any postcode.

Kieran Johnson

Two Reservations

I *Moonshine and French Dressing*

With bubbles brewing, steaming,
there's only briefly speaking.

Your olive skin's intriguing,
the vinegar of your tongue.

You stand all night, dreaming,
to catch the moon-glow, sleeping.

She waits for you and beaming,
will eat you with a spoon.

II *Too Slow to Simmer*

Oh, foreplay? Yes, more play –
it's hard to hold you down.
You spike me, delight me,
whenever you come to town.

Where keep you?
Or sleep? You –
so seldom come around.

Replay me, fillet me –
bring steak and red wine, too.
Just take me, then make me
sweet-savory for you.

But keep? You?
Or sleep? You –
too seldom can be found.

Suzanne Johanson

Egg and Soldier

You did knock -
I'll give you that much.
A silver spooned seduction.

Splintered my shell
took my head clean off,
scooped out my conscience.

Fingers sank in,
licked clean, came again,
moved through the depths of me.

Scraped my sides,
scratched every last
softened sliver from me.

Once emptied
your hands cupped me,
considered crushing me.

Instead, a child's trick –
turned me upside down.
From the outside I'm perfect.

Perfectly hollow.
Do not come knocking again,
I would shatter at first touch.

Nicola Beaumont

Resolution

This new year's day, soft and slow,
snow falls across the hills
like a veil or a new vow,

deadening distant churchbells,
as we set out on our walk,
to low, dull mumbles

until larch and birch and oak
soak up the last drops of sound.
Neither of us speak,

but you seek my hand
in the pocket of my coat,
and I feel your knuckles bend

awkwardly in search of the old fit.
Snow falls, slow and soft,
thickening underfoot,

as I untangle fingers deftly,
mutter about being off the path,
and let my thoughts drift

like the sough of our breath
in midwinter air;
and silently I restate the myth

that a cool and civil veneer,
like a crust of frost, staunches
faithlessness. Near and far,

snow falls: by evening, ten inches
block our tracks from view
and burden the branches.

Kieran Johnson

Bed

The night's a bitten tongue.
It's swelling cannot be contained
by the tea-lights
placed around our bed
like dead lanterns.

You approach by dark
a need for kisses.
Wet with fear,
they make me hate you
as much as me.

A joke would help,
but now there is only
turning away. Burrowing down.
While my body desiccates,
I keep absolutely still.

Richard Moorhead

Wife

her day so numb
until she pricks
her thumb so red
it must be true

beneath this prim
and silent cloth
there brims a tide
of blood and love –

and down around
beyond as wine
unzips it slips
the binding ring

and free she turns
her hand to find
the river lines
of all she was

she was and will
no longer be –
her thumb so red
it must be true.

Phil Wood

Aubade for Edith Sitwell

Daybreak tumbles down the stair,
slips, and soaks my ragged hair.

Morning light, relentless rain
turn out tilted tunes again;

plainsong of the wind, perchance –
(overtones in solemn dance)?

Wooden flowers and stodgy kale
stage this cockscomb-crazy tale

where your gaucho lover waits,
drenched in horsesweat, by the gates.

He'll lose courage. It's not fair;
Edith, Edith, leave him there.

(Creaking timbers dip and slide,
mirrors crack from side to side.)

Must you have him, broom and gorse?
Very well. I'll take his horse.

Tracks of birds' feet in the sky
beat full-heavy drums, but I

travel light, ride bareback. Gone.
Looped into the rising sun.

Send a message, spin a wheel.
Paint a promise. Daub a deal.

Jane Røken

Picasso's Garden

for Dora Maar

I draw him as he sleeps. He tears from my skin
like a necessary thorn, directs which way my limbs
will bend; how pungent the scent of each blossom.

He plants me next to hollyhocks and winged seeds
of pine, places his paint brush in the tomato can
and demands I grow near wisteria. I witness her shells

in the breeze; how she dabs the perfume of mauve water
between her legs, offers him the sympathy
of a dandelion. In Spring, a peony tempts him

with her red fist. He will part her like a cheap carnation
and there's nothing I can do about it. I was born with a nub
that will not open, a womb blank as a canvas. He says

we all must sacrifice. But I stop giving it away, shut down
my nectar and bury its scent. He swallows me anyway,
like thistles of burdock, makes me believe

he loves my bitterness. I endure the scent of peat on his lips,
pack his brushes and pretend he is leaving but we carry
one another's seed. He will chase me into the afterlife.

Oh where is my mouth? I think of silence, how difficult
for a weed to speak. This is the profile I must not sketch –
hornets humming along the edge of his jaw.

Lois P. Jones

Pantone: 1665 C

It is kumquats for Keats
and a celebration in couplets.

The Happy Birthday you won't sing me
and the candles I won't have.

It was seeing June in 1994
slumbering through an endless summer.

Tuesdays were clementines and liqueur
burning a stream-bed along the path of the throat.

Teeth cracking the Jaffa cake crust
releasing a tang as thick as lava to the tongue.

It was the first dress I ever brought you
still sitting in the wardrobe unworn.

The walks down Via dei Fori Imperiali
the sun burning off the wall

and that sunset in Paris
trellised through the Eiffel Tower.

It was the day you told me
and I sat lost within the wash of it.

Do you remember Frigiliana
and reaching out to pick the perfect fruit?

Ben Johnson

Ways to Paint a Woman

> *A handful sleepcorn drifts from the mouth*
> *stammered true out towards the snow conversations.* ~ Paul Celan

Sometimes you cannot say
what is in the heart.

Sometimes you have to paint it yellow –
listen with the eyes: honeycomb and maize,

golden rain flowers.
Transform with your softest brush

the way Lorca's bathing girl liquifies
into water – half a head in fire,

sun burning a trail
from forehead to cheek. Graze

the mouth with mango.
Make time blend and take away.

Use the green of a blind man
when he says *you're beautiful*

and means *you're timeless*. Show
what the light gave her

washing warmth into a neck
until it's a dune, a cliffside

that holds a head of surf. Paint

as you would before you awaken,

when sunlight falls like milkweed
and you are an empty silo

letting her grain fill you – buttery malt
and biscuit, for the love of honey.

Lois P. Jones

At the Kawamura Museum of Art, with Children

1. An Introduction to Chagall

That fish is not a fish but a crayon
the artist designed for drawing rainbows,
and the whole thing is a candy bar.

Except the marzipan goats of course
and the King in the corner cut from icing.
If we stuck straws in this nocturnal background

we could suck the juice right out of the canvas,
blow bubbles through the petals of floating bouquets,
ruffle the feathers of airbourne poultry.

Maybe stir the flames of this candelabra,
illuminate the face of the hidden painter
crouched in youth behind his easel.

I'd urge him pack his colours and grab
the other end. We'd pull him from his dream.
You could show him the cracks

where the black has been lifted,
point to the ledge of the sun where a child
paints the world with rainbows, rainbows.

2. Rembrandt's Man in a Broad-Brimmed Hat

I'm less impressed with the hat
than the beard. Such fine strokes

you must enjoy in your stone walled chamber,
where intricate shadows cast by candlelight

reveal as much as they conceal. I envy
the frills that dance with your bristles,

leaning this way and that with each turn
of your head, bowing like servants as you glare,

rising like soldiers when you reach for a thought.
The hat and its matching velvet cape,

warm enough to pink your cheeks, speak
of privilege. You do not bow or rise for others.

All these textures are but leaves
of an artichoke – peel away, peel away,

peel away until the eyes glisten,
wet, raw and unflinching, following us

around the room, out the door,
all the way home and under our beds.

3. *Rothko*

Imagine allowing a child to run
around inside a broken human heart.

Broken, that is, in the mechanical sense,
with cogs and cylinders strewn about,

loose wires that trip, screws that snag,
protruding springs that might draw blood.

What else would a child do in such a room
but gather up the various parts

and assemble something new. Attach nouns
to abstract shapes, find windows of meaning

where before there were none. When finished
they'd step back to assess their work, grab

the sleeve of any nearby adult, point
and say: *Look. What's this?*

Brian Edwards

Necessity

I make sure you eat breakfast
on most days.

I call you my man-cub,
read you overdue books
past your bed time.

You choose our secret word,
ketchup, the code to be broken
by anyone who ever comes for you
in my name.

I introduce you to the animal kingdom.
He comes sniffing around for me,
never stays long, twists your arm,
roughs your hair on his way out.
You tell me he smells.

After school you create things
like melting cheese on Ritz crackers
in the microwave; inventing
the scene where your body hugs
the wall so your shadow
won't slide beneath the door.

I am late again, with no word sent.

You press your face against
the fish eye lens
so you can see
in every direction.

Jane Loechler

Yin and Yang

When I was little, Dad explained to me
the meaning of my name: the first character,
firm on the ground; the next two,
dazzling vermilion. Thus, a land
under the reflection of a red sun.

When I grew up, I learned
how he, with a deep-rooted
southern accent, pronounced land
as green, that sets off the rebirth
of flowers in a bird chirping spring
along a thousand miles of riverbanks.

Now, I place red and green side by side,
like two fish swimming head to tail in a globe,
where I see moonrise and sunset,
west wind chasing east rain,
and rivers embracing mountains.

Lucy Lu

Appletree

The tree I planted,
near thirty autumns ago,
has long since grown above
the protective hedge
that kept it
from the withering north winds.

Choking weeds
that once threatened
can only look up.

It lost its leaves of inexperience,
and slowly pushed out
small branches of knowledge,
bearing early blossom.
The fruit, hard and sour,
was left where it fell.

In time the tree soaked up wisdom,
a sweetness of life,
its blossom no longer just
a fine dress
for youth's bitterness.

Now, far away from this tree,
I feel happy knowing that it grows,
still blooms,
even though
I am no longer there to see it.

Barrie Haughton

Haugh Lane

1.
Those yellow stones changed colour in the rain.
And what precipitation we would suffer:
the hands of sycamores pressing against
the slate-grey sky in vain, while slabs of butter
dulled to day-old toast. Pigeons and sparrows,
denied the camouflage of wilder species,
reliant on the town's gutters and furrows,
dispersed to copses, nested under eaves:
the bakery, the school, the mill, the church
all unsuspecting bustle. Come the sun
then come the green, the effervescent burn
of earth. Top of the town, the steeple shone,
a suggestion that religion quarries best
where nature reigns and education rests.

2.
With its foreign parts, like vestibule and alcove,
the house enriched my lexicon with names.
I'd forgotten we had money then. Dad drove
a Volvo, and Mum shopped at C & A.
The cellar housed a games room, we had wicker
furniture in the kitchen and an open
coal fire in the lounge, with tongs and pokers
hanging by the hearth, wrought from iron
and fashioned into figures of medieval
knights. I loved their weight and heft, the coolness
in my hand, the thud and clatter when they fell.
I watched them plunge deep down into the furnace,
the cinerator, the crucible, the grate,
excavating grails of light and heat.

3.
Never a full chorus, not even a verse.
Sometimes a couplet, but mostly just a line,
his sudden, fitful a capella bursts
were lights flicked on and off inside his mind,
Catherine wheels, cocked and knocked askew
firing off their lyrical constellations
at random. Names of girls or towns he once knew,
a distant life, one never forgotten.
He would disappear beneath his soap and brush,
then re-emerge, always naked to the waist,
with all his teeth, pomaded, Old-Spice-splashed,
with tissue Japanese flags on his face
and that map of Ireland birth-mark on his back
as red and huge and permanent as the past.

4.
Almost three decades have passed and still
the same red cheeks, the dryness round the mouth,
relaying how I would drag her up that hill
to make it home in time for Danger Mouse.
And every time she tells it there's a slight
embellishment, a detail lost or gained:
the bus perhaps an extra minute late,
an inside-out umbrella in the rain.
And each time is more difficult than the last
to hear, our whole relationship condensed
to a sugar cube. I urge her to relate
her thirty-something body, her muscles tense
and taut, the burning in her calves and thighs,
the breathlessness, the windows rich with eyes.

5.
We'd climb into our Dad's parked car and rock
it back and forth, imitating with our mouths
the sounds of freedom, declaring our next stop
London, with just an inkling it was South
of Manchester. Sometimes we'd fool our friends
that we were really moving, that we could drive,
perfecting the illusion of a bend,
a three-point turn, the speed of traffic lights.
Our older brother drove a Ford Capri,
with racing stripes, a black metallic finish,
spotlights, spoilers, bucket seats, and a CB
crackling out its alien forms of English:
Breaker, Breaker. Copy, are you reading?
How many candles are you burning?

Brian Edwards

Crook the Gardener (1786-1991)

I have seen him,
quiet, hedged in solitude,
content in well-marked
and tended ground.
He moves to a once unknown purpose,
that I now glimpse.
Dad knew him.
Granddad knew him like a brother.
Great-granddad leans, easy in old sepia,
photographed by the sweet peas,
and there, also by his side,
is Crook the gardener, older than us all.

I only know he saw me limping.
His words, simple enough,
would once have met a busy deafness.
Said before, now said to me:
"Come out into my garden
it makes me happy.
All my planted things have grown.
Little comes to much in life.
Much comes to little. But there,
all my planted things have grown."

Seth Crook

The War of Attrition

When the dog no more remembered
where yesterday's bones were buried,
the old gal began conversing
with her long-dead mother and father.

When his eyesight blurred and during walks
he attached himself to strangers
she wrote off to Her Majesty
claiming blue-blooded connections.

At night he would lose his bearings
and come barking into bedrooms;
she rang the railway and requested
a Return to 1940.

He grew too slow for sticks we'd throw
and deaf to our exhortations;
she wedged into a wheelchair tuned
to the BBC Home Service.

We finally had the dog put down,
he was buried in the garden;
she wore best togs and waved a flag
at the VE Celebrations.

Ray Miller

Boarding

In her nineties she begins to daydream
shrugging off the rug and velcroed slippers
to dig her toes in the tumbled strandline

of the residents' lounge. Standing,
she watches while the morning swishes up
around her, noisy with the squawk

of what she thinks are oystercatchers
dressed in black and white
and the long-stretched necks of gannets

cramming food and squabbling. She walks
to the water's edge where clothes are piled
in heaps. Here are boards, leaning

on the breakwater, and she flicks one upright
with a practised foot, drags it down the beach
to deeper water. The sand's the shade of early morning

tea. She tosses bread into the sky
to get a feeling for the breeze, manoeuvres
so the sail is downwind of the nurses

skimming through the corridor towards her.
Surf's high. She heaves her stern-ward hand
hard against the boom to pull away.

Rosemary Badcoe

Taking Out Grandma

The Rest Home staff are mostly Filipinos,
though they look like Vietnam:
there's an arm in a sling, a neck in a brace,
her name is a flinch on a foreign face.
She hasn't attacked for a day and a half
but the unspoken pact is easily snapped.
By inches she dies, by strokes she vanishes;
our fingers are crossed for a final push –
not the Long March but the Apocalypse.

A Brass Band plays in the Winter Gardens
each Sunday of the summer.
We sit underneath the handkerchief tree,
half an ear for approaching thunder
and half an eye on the spiteful sky;
she spills tea and bemoans the weather,
partly here, part music hall era.
When the first fat drops of rain land
the band play Over The Rainbow
without a stumble in their schedule,
as if the world had some agenda.
She sings – sings with such fragility,
that all those who share our shelter
join in to lift and help her.
Handkerchiefs float around our eyes
disturbed by weight of water.

Ray Miller

Still Chartreuse

The lantern glows pale yellow.
Denial reads the paper
and doesn't say a word.
Doesn't check the clock,
doesn't herald the forecast
or listen for sounds
of a waking house.
Denial sits in pale yellow.

But the forest floor
is still chartreuse.
The yellow of death
hasn't fully leached
the green out of the ferns;
there's a neon patchwork of moss
bordering blood-red blueberry leaves
and there is still time to gather.

And the morning sky is a blue page
of airmail stationery
and the birch trees wave
faded yellow stamps
in the October wind.
And it's easy to pretend
she's still in her room.

Suzanne Johanson

Split Second

0.18 When you think you have recognised someone's voice

The whisper is a husk of rice,
it lies within a broken cup
of instant ice.

Evaporates in a finger-click.
It makes me wonder,
was it even there?

0.45 When the ink spreads too much on soft paper

The scratch of air's calligraphy.
The pen with ink on paper
thick enough to drain
a fish-fin filigree into linen.

The capillaries are thin as time
and spread the slimness that it takes
your eye to register the movement
of the spreading black.

0.67 Suddenly you smell woodsmoke

You notice Winter
glassy, with the air all nice

in the nose. Its razor
slits the bleach of brightness,
then sacrifices bulbs of blood
like this:

the way the nose is instant
when it smells smoke.

1.00 The point at which it becomes evening

When the clean light has gone
from the air and in its place,
the throats of woodsmoke
hang on ruddy twilight, pelts
of daylight, shrunk.

1.23 Gone

The way your Mother
always said, I should
take more care of you.
The way she said,
I should take more care.
The way she gestured
to watch for the signs.

Richard Moorhead

Bottom Dead Centre

Intake

Ice-path uncles, sliding, come
to top-up stockings, sip sherry,
be knocked unconscious by the Queen.
The old year has been dripping
through the cracks in December,
now only one festival remains.

Compression

Fewer and smaller,
the uncles left for us to visit
dribbling in their rest-homes.
What troupe remains to get festive?
To turn up, unexpected? To decorate the tree
and give you socks?

Combustion

I give you socks
to wear outside your boots
wending from the crematorium
with the path caked in icing, decoration
a drain-pipe dribbled through its crack.
We spontaneously scatter Uncle Clive.

Exhaust

All the uncles scattered once,
when you aced and raced the new sled
of simpler years. Now the pagan tree
is baubed with tears, as you tear the ribbon-paper.
Another pair of socks – useful. At our age
the ritual differs. The engine hesitates,
one year unsafely dead, and drawing-in
one drawn-out breath we wait
to long-live the new.

Ian Badcoe

Snettisham

This is the Wash it seems –
a last exhalation
of the dying land, or something
the sea's been working on
for ages: sketching it in,
rubbing it out,
redoing and redoing it,
never satisfied.

Look at you, all wrapped up,
hat and scarf and
gloves, and those wild eyes
made weak by medication
and hopes confounded so
so many times.
Never this thin before.
Going slowly, in this
flattest part of England,
going slowly downhill.

The birds rise
like a handful of rain
thrown upward,

and the Great Twitcher
in the sky misses
nothing. His fondness
for sparrows is well known.

David Callin

Omniscient

Mind's eye's momentarily
blinded by the half-brick bouncing
off the upstairs window, shattering
the Sunday evening lethargy –
an unscriptured break in "Songs of Praise".

Adrenalin overcomes the stairs,
two at a time, finds no
holes in glass or wallet but
outside on the flat
roof, lies a little bird, inert,
flew into mirrors
masquerading as the twilight air.

Concern opens windows, steps
out onto silver spongey-feeling felt
– check if it's dead (she says)
– can't leave it, living, for
the Cat-Next-Door.

Hunter-gatherer goes
down on all fours, extends
a clumsy, clammy hand –
What life remains within
the bird erupts on
desperate, despairing wings,
staggers round in
heart-breaking circles,
subsides, receding fast.

Inadequacy enfolds the
bird, hopes warm hands might
somehow heal but knows
he's merely holding
on, until the end of
the film that slowly
forms on dimming eyes.

We all of me bear
witness to the little death,
knowing that somewhere, unseen,
Next-Door's Cat sees all.

Geoff Blanchard

On the Down Line

—a descent of some type,
such as moving downhill,
or the sinking of the winds
or sun,
a military retreat,
or a trip to the underworld
or a trip from the interior of a country
down to the coast.—Wikipedia—"*Katabasis*"

Would a figure figure in the ending
of the trip? Tired and how archaic,
a gate-warden, perhaps, who spits
half-chewed tobacco,
the spittle flying, off-stage
from the light he has raised
in one arthritic hand
into some outer darkness
to form tiny settlements
of dying, congealing mucus
on a stone so far beyond
mortal concern
that no dust gathers.
And if he had some sort of vehicle,
this warden,
a traditional boat, or perhaps a charabanc
engined in oil and antiquity, and glimmering brass pipes;

if there was such a vehicle
would you take a place
on age-riddled, half-cracked seating? Would you
hesitate at the risk of meeting an old friend
who in later life you came to never like,
or a cleaning woman, freshly slain but not yet
laid out in her beeswax and lavender
encrusted duster? Would you fear the general muster
of folk a touch too keen to chance another world,
having nothing from the last?

Or would you, knowing your place,
take the space between a rapist,
and a collector of second-hand ties;
face forward and grip your expectant ticket so firmly
that your sweat – cold as must be –
will print a ragged patch on the cheap cardboard;
wait for the old man's creaking arm
to pull hard on the handbrake; and wait again
to hear one final, semi-comic honking
from his rubber-bulb horn?

Ian Badcoe

Drowning Doesn't Look Like Drowning

She had it wrong, the girl who thought
she knew waving from drowning,
could tell the edge of life from its middle,
see shape and bone change to the flat
of ocean. Drowning is the desperate quiet,
the body pinned upright, the line
where sea meets air.

Those who yell and splash still have time
for speech, to strike a bargain with a wave,
debate the motion of the tides.
Look instead for ones who gaze at you
with blinded eyes, already treading
some internal stair; climbing a ladder
that isn't there.

Rosemary Badcoe

King Alfred's Cakes

They cling beneath the dying ash, a troop
of mourners shucked in black. Each year
another cerecloth forms and serves to hide
the primal spore. Paternal growth becomes
entombed within itself; but when exhumed,
the grey concentric feathered rings, once spewed
of ink, rekindle long dead flames again
and raze the ancient tree to ash.

John C. Nash

Just Make Sure

I must insist no prayers
are read
when I am dead (or just before),
and what's more, I ask you, please,
don't dress in black,
wear a death mask,
or hold back. Just have a drink,
enjoy the crack. Be wary of
persistent priests
with rumours that I
rest in peace. Don't talk of any good I did,
stand your beer
on my coffin lid – remember
I could be a twat – so don't forget
to mention that.
Play my music
good and loud, dress me
in a hippy shroud, and when they feed me
to the ground, make sure that there's
no scratching sound.

Barrie Haughton

Appendices

INDEX OF FIRST LINES AND TITLES

(Titles are shown in italics and first lines are shown in plain type. Some of the first lines have been truncated).

...and then there was the time I was up against Armitage. 56
0.18 When you think you have recognised......................93
A fawn, I thought at first: a sylvan scene,........................31
A Secret Hobby..23
A thin sheen of frost glitters in the beam........................ 37
Above the beach are horses, or so we must believe,..........39
Across a pale December sky,... 62
Agua Potable.. 60
Angels Writing to the Hebrides...................................61
Appletree... 84
At the Kawamura Museum of Art.................................79
Aubade for Edith Sitwell..74
Baker...49
Bed...72
Bells send time onto the hillside after me.......................41
Blanking...34
Boarding.. 90
Borderland, Shadowgate.. 40
Bottom Dead Centre...95
By the Book..54
By the Rising of the Moon...22
Corner Shop Cocktails... 66
Crisis.. 16
Crook the Gardener..88
Daybreak tumbles down the stair,...................................74
Dead Pubs of Douglas.. 64
Drowning Doesn't Look Like Drowning......................102
Easter Sunday is the day I associate with you,.................67

Eating for Two	*28*
Egg and Soldier	*69*
Elementary Catastrophe Theory	*14*
Feeding Time	*30*
Feel Sorry for Mercury	*15*
for consciousness in cephalopods	25
From the larder, mother, behind the door	49
Fugit	*39*
Gull	*27*
Haugh Lane	*85*
her day so numb	73
How close to sense his responses are,	18
How Hebridean Sheep Walk in the Rain	*63*
I draw him as he sleeps. He tears from my skin	75
I have seen him,	88
I make sure you eat breakfast	82
I must insist no prayers	104
I wake with the dawn and the fall	36
I'm less impressed with the hat	80
I'm starting to wonder what is going on around here	17
Ice-path uncles, sliding, come	95
Imagine allowing a child to run	81
In her nineties she begins to daydream	90
Intense as a conspiracy, coiled	58
It is kumquats for Keats	76
Just Make Sure	*104*
King Alfred's Cakes	*103*
Leaning over the old bridge,	30
Let us suppose a is alone, at equilibrium,	14
Long before they came to me they slipped off	53
Madam,	61
Making Contact	*20*
Mark well this moment	43
Mind's eye momentarily	98
Mishearings	*31*

Morning Over Chibbanagh 62
Mussels 26
My Arguments 25
My Next Film 59
Necessity 82
Never a full chorus, not even a verse 86
Not everyone has words they need to say 20
Oblique Ascension 11
Omniscient 98
On a chair built for vaudeville 60
On the Down Line 100
On the forty-first day of the nineteenth month 47
On the tap-end 52
Ouija 12
Outlines 20
Pantone: 1665 C 76
Parked up by a wringing wood 16
Piange oggi? I'd reached 33
Piangere 33
Picasso's Garden 75
Pilgrim's Journal 47
pock-marked 15
Pomegrenades 44
Rather Cerebral Conceptual Graffiti Artists 17
Rejection does not make you a bad poet 57
Resolution 70
Shall I mourn your decline with some ad-hoc wine? ... 66
She had it wrong, the girl who thought 102
She reads books, ... 54
Slow Cooker 50
Snettisham 97
Sometimes you cannot say 77
Split Second 93
Still Chartreuse 92
T.S.Eliot Takes the Turing Test 18

Table	*51*
Taking Out Grandma	*91*
Tales from the Bareknuckle Poet	*56*
That fish is not a fish but a crayon	79
The Collar	*41*
The Concert	*58*
The Dripping Tap	*52*
The lantern glows pale yellow	92
The Modified Behavior of Fruit	*45*
The motherland can tell	45
The New Life	*67*
The night's a bitten tongue	72
The old woman picked "Pomegrenades"	*44*
The past's engrained	51
The Rest Home staff are mostly Filipinos,	91
The roofs of cars	34
The sea is hard on you - the way	26
The Sloven's Assistant	*53*
The tree I planted,	84
The War of Attrition	*89*
The Year of Horses	*37*
They cling beneath the dying ash, a troop	103
This is the Wash it seems -	97
This new year's day, soft and slow,	70
This poem is not about you, in the same way	11
Those yellow stones changed colour in the rain	85
Threshold Days	*43*
Today i want to say something wonderful	50
Twenty-two laborious hours,	28
Two Reservations	*68*
Unaware of the fact that they would never meet,	40
Warmed only by the dye on their backs,	63
Ways to Paint a Woman	*77*
We craft stories to tell	20
We keep hinges in a jar shelved and sealed,	23

We will not start..64	
We'd climb into our Dad's parked car and rock...............87	
When I was little, Dad explained to me..........................83	
When push and shove come, at last,............................. 28	
When the dog no more remembered.............................89	
White...*36*	
Who Hangs the Rabbits..*24*	
Wife.. *73*	
will have a bearded left wing protagonist......................59	
With bubbles brewing, steaming,.................................. 68	
Would a figure figure in the ending.............................100	
Write. Do it slowly, as if you're riding a secret language;... 22	
Yin and Yang..*83*	
You asked for an R, for the ripening of olives................... 12	
You did knock -... 69	
You, the lone fool.. 27	
Zen and the Art of Submitting Poetry........................ *57*	

BIOGRAPHIES

Since you are already acquainted with the poems here are a few words about the poets behind them. Each poet's name is followed by their user name on Poets' Graves Forum to make it easier to find more of their work.

Ian Badcoe (Bodkin)

Ian lives in Sheffield and walks on the moors, returning to the city occasionally for essential supplies, such as money. He has been published in WordAid's *Did I Tell You?* and *Not Only the Dark* anthologies, and in the excellent *Antiphon*, on-line magazine.

Rosemary Badcoe (Ros)

Rosemary walks the moors and argues about the nature of consciousness. She is currently undertaking the MA Writing at Sheffield Hallam University. She has been published in various magazines and anthologies, most recently *Fourteen Magazine*, *Orbis* and *Other Poetry* and is editor of the online poetry magazine *Antiphon* http://antiphon.org.uk and moderator of the poetry forum Poets' Graves.

Nicola Beaumont (Nicky B)

Nicola is Lancashire born and bred but is currently displaced in South Devon. Her day job is as a marine scientist and she has published extensively in the scientific literature. This is her poetic debut.

Nicola reads and writes most days and attends spoken word events whenever possible, including the regular "Forked" poetry night. She has recently weaned herself off an obsession with strict rhythm and rhyme, and with the help of the Poets' Graves forum she believes she may be slowly improving.

Geoff Blanchard (twoleftfeet)

Geoff is a retired computer programmer from the dinosaur days of mainframe computers. He lives in East London and spends his time struggling to come to terms with personal computers, anything else that doesn't run on clockwork, the impossibility of getting a guitar to stay in tune for longer than 2 minutes, and tai chi.

Lia Brooks (Lia)

Lia, twice nominated for the *Pushcart Prize*, has poems published in various magazines and journals in the UK and the US. Some of these include; *Poetry London, Lily Lit Review, California Quarterly, Magma Poetry* newsletters, *Qarrtsiluni, American Poetry Journal, Loch Raven Review* and *Penumbra*. She was short-listed for the *New Leaf Short Poetry Prize* and has been part of two ekphrastic events in collaboration with painters in Indiana and California. She was born in Surrey and now lives in Southampton, UK, with her partner and two sons.

David Callin (David)

David Callin lives on one of Britain's offshore islands but not, regrettably, for tax reasons. *Cha nel monney Gaelg echey*. His poems have appeared in *The Journal, Orbis* and *Envoi* among others, and in a number of online magazines, including *Message in a Bottle, Snakeskin* and *Antiphon*.

Seth Crook (Antcliff)

Seth Crook lives in the Hebrides and taught philosophy at various universities in the US before homesickness got the better of him. One day he found that fragments of family history were turning into poems. He hasn't stopped writing since. He doesn't like cod philosophy in poetry, but likes cod, philosophy and poetry. His work has been published this year in *Other Poetry, Ink, Sweat and Tears, Snakeskin, Antiphon, The Centrifugal Eye, Message in a Bottle, The Journal, Poetry Scotland* (*Open Mike*) and *Northwords Now*.

Brian Edwards (brianedwards)

Brian Edwards, an Englishman, lives in Japan. His work has most recently appeared in *Other Poetry, Envoi, 14, Orbis, Antiphon* and *Snakeskin*. He is currently working on a collaboration with Black Stripe Theater, a company which produces and performs English language theatre in Tokyo. He is a founding editor at After Literature (afterliterature.org). His first poetry collection is expected to appear in 2013.

John Glennon (John G)

John was born in London and migrated to Yorkshire with his family in tow. He tends to write his poems during the commute to a faceless office full of humming computers. By means of poetry he attempts to poke a finger at the human condition while remaining funny, irreverent and enjoyable to read. There is a further selection of John's work available at http://eatmorewords.wordpress.com

Barrie Haughton (barrie)

Barrie was born and raised in Leigh, Lancashire. He was often in trouble at school and it was on one of these occasions, after being sent out of class and to the library, that he discovered a book of poetry. It became his passion. He was particularly interested in poetry from the First World War and it was his love of Wordsworth that led him to settle in the Lake District with his family. Barrie contracted emphysema a little after his fiftieth birthday and was unable to venture outdoors much after that. It was writing poetry and the positive comments from others on the forum that kept him going during those years. In January 2009 Barrie finally succumbed to his illness but his poems are still loved.

Suzanne Johanson (Suzanne)

Suzanne in an American living in Finland with her husband. Trained in Recreational Leadership, she works at an international kindergarten where she sings, dances, enjoys hugs and nurtures laughter. Her weekends are spent in the forest as often as possible. Her favorite activities include riding her mountain bike, lifting weights and relaxing with her husband. She is an artist who quilts, crochets and hand-builds ceramic sculptures.

When she began writing poetry in 2006, she discovered her passion for word games and her interest in interpersonal communication could be entwined. She continues to find satisfaction in wrestling with putting a message into a concise poetic form. Her work often deals with the intimate relationship between two people.

Ben Johnson (BenJohnson)

Ben lives on the edge of the New Forest close to the sea. By day he is an IT Administrator but outside working hours he aspires to writing poetry. During secondary education he was repeatedly told by his English teacher not to write in rhyme, advice which he ignored for years. Since coming to the Poets' Graves forums he has learnt to be more flexible in his approach to writing.

For several years he dreamt about setting up a poetry publishing venture and finally realised in 2012 that there was nothing to stop him doing so.

Kieran Johnson (k-j)

Kieran Johnson has lived in the UK, Canada and the USA. He is married with two children and employed as a chartered accountant. He enjoys oysters, bicycles, music and literature.

Lois P. Jones (emuse)

Lois is radio host for "Poet's Café" (KPFK, Los Angeles 90.7 fm), and co-produces Monday West and Moonday East's poetry readings in Pacific Palisades and La Cañada, Flintridge, California with Alice Pero. She is the Poetry Editor of *Kyoto Journal* and as of 2012, a four-time Pushcart nominee. She has poetry published in *American Poetry Journal, Qarrtsiluni, Sierra Nevada Review, Askew, Raven Chronicles, Tiferet, Antioch University's Lunch Ticket* as well as *Destinations*, the number one jazz CD in the U.S. (Tamir Hendelman, 2010) and other journals in the U.S. and abroad. Several of her photographs have been published in national journals.

Lois's poems have won honors under judges Kwame Dawes, Fiona Sampson and others. New Yorker staff writer, Dana Goodyear selected "Ouija" as Poem of the Year in the 2010 competition sponsored by Web Del Sol. She is the winner of the 2012 Tiferet Poetry Prize and will be featured in The Tiferet Talk Interviews, which includes interviews with Robert Pinsky, Julia Cameron and others forthcoming winter 2012.

David Kelly (oranggunung)

David was a baby boomer who grew up in ignorance of "Howl" and beat poetry. As a child, He was captivated by the peculiar verses of Lear, Carroll, Belloc and Milligan, but preferred to hear it read rather than read it himself. Following a self-appraisal of the outpourings of teenage angst, he decided that his poetry was probably best kept private. He trained as a zoologist and aspired to be published in scientific journals.

With a little persuasion from his nephew, in the New Year of 2007, he started to write again. This opened the floodgates to a random assortment of poems. Having no formal training, he was tempted to try and create the peculiar poems that he had heard as a child. It wasn't until he joined Poets' Graves (later in 2007) that he found the guidance that led him to experiment with other forms. Currently, most of his efforts are directed towards haiku, tanka and haibun.

Jane Loechler (Wilcken)

Jane is a poet and sculptor living in St. Paul, Minnesota. She received her BFA from the Minneapolis College of Art & Design and has poems published or forthcoming in *Bat City Review, Elimae, Camroc Press Review, PANK Magazine* and *Burntdistrict*.

Lucy Lu (Lake)

Lucy lives in Minnesota, the land of ten thousand lakes. Her passion for poetry (now drawing) flickers through her many years living in a diverse culture, that calls for a fresh look at things happening around us. She enjoys teaching in a language school during the weekend more than her full time job.

Ray Miller (ray miller)

Ray lives in a pink house with a wife and too many children. Then there's the dogs, cats, rabbit, mice, hamsters, guinea-pigs, frogs, Giant African Land Snails, fish and snakes. He puts it down to very bad karma.

He sees himself somewhere between T.S.Eliot and George Formby and only slightly more alive than they. He's done performance poetry. Never once booed off stage, often booed on. He has a Worst Enemy List and is only in 3rd place at the moment, but he hasn't given up yet.

Richard Moorhead (Pleiades)

Richard Moorhead splits his time between London and Cardiff. His poetry has appeared in *Magma, Mimesis, Antiphon, Anon, the Financial Times* and various anthologies *Sea Pie* (Shearsman Books); *Adventures in Form* (Penned in the Margin); *Not only the Dark* (WorldAid/Shelterbox). His pamphlet, *The Reluctant Vegetarian* (Oystercatcher Press), was shortlisted for the Michael Marks Poetry Prize.

John C. Nash (Nash)

John finally settled down as a self-employed bookbinder and writer in Northampton, UK. His work has been published in various online and in-print magazines including *Antiphon, Triggerfish, The Delinquent, Cake and Ink, Sweat & Tears*.

Jane Røken (Magpie Jane)

Jane is Norwegian, lives in Denmark, and likes to think of herself as an internationalist. She has been writing poetry as well as prose since childhood, mostly in an erratic and rather unsystematic way. Her writings have been published in several online magazines, such as *Antiphon, Mobius, Snakeskin, Shit Creek Review*, and *Astropoetica*. Besides reading and writing, she enjoys gardening, photography, and roughhiking with her husband. Now approaching pension age, she has been working in many different trades, but has not yet decided what she wants to be when she grows up. Until then, she keeps on writing.

Cameron Self (Cameron)

Cameron was born in Cambridge in 1962 and moved to Poringland in Norfolk in 1964. He studied Geography at Hull University from 1980-83 and then an MA in Creative Writing at Lancaster University 1984-5.

He has had poems published in the *Faber Book of Blue Verse, Poetry Review, Rialto, Iron* and *Outposts Quarterly*. My first collection of poetry '*Gedney Drove End*' was shortlisted for the East Anglian Book Awards in 2010.

Cameron is also the author of the 'Poets' Graves' and 'Literary Norfolk' websites.

Kris Thain (camus)

Kris lives in a seaside town that forgot to close down, and often takes advantage of that. The desolate shoreline is a great inspiration for knocking out a few poems. He web-designs by day, he web-designs by night and hopes one day to stop the night part and live a "normal" life.

He has travelled to Vietnam, Cambodia, Thailand and India and knows full well these are the countries we should model ourselves on. He has two children: Lori and Lou who are great.

He is 40 odd. He has had poems published in *Other Poetry, Snakeskin, Orbis* and two lesser known local publications.

Phil Wood (Macavity)

Phil prefers to let his poetry do the talking for him.

Marc Woodward (Marc)

Marc Woodward has contributed poetry to a number of printed journals and online sites as well as performing live and on radio broadcasts. Much of his work reflects his home environment in rural Devon and he draws on influences as diverse as Edward Thomas, Phillip Larkin, and William Carlos Williams. He seeks beauty in structure but finds it to be in constant contest with economy and simplicity!

Marc is also a highly regarded mandolinist who has performed with well known acts on the UK folk and blues scene, and he has released and featured on a number of recordings. Keen eyed TV viewers may also have seen him presenting daytime TV on

BBC1 - clearly poetry and mandolin-ing doesn't pay as well as it might... You can find more of Marc's poetry online http://marcwoodwardpoetry.blogspot.co.uk/

CREDITS

We would like to thank Sam Webster for allowing us to use her photograph *Falling Leaves* for the front cover of this book.

Sam has a degree in Fine Art Sculpture and Art History. Her photographic work has appeared in film, television and as album sleeve art. She works predominantly in black and white and is influenced by the works of early 20th Century cinematographers.

If you wish to discover more of Sam's work there is a selection viewable at http://www.etsy.com/shop/SamWebsterPhoto

We also wish to thank the generosity and dedication of the following Open Source teams; **Scribus, Libre Office, GIMP** and **Inkscape**. These products are helping to change the face of software by bringing professional quality products into the reach of everyone. This book has been produced using only Open Source software.

Lightning Source UK Ltd.
Milton Keynes UK
UKOW052300210113

205178UK00005B/794/P

9 780957 185210